Silent
WARFARE

MARY TERTEROV

BALBOA.PRESS
A DIVISION OF HAY HOUSE

Balboa Press books may be ordered through booksellers or by contacting:

Balboa Press
A Division of Hay House
1663 Liberty Drive
Bloomington, IN 47403
www.balboapress.com
844-682-1282

Print information available on the last page.

ISBN: 979-8-7652-5002-0 (sc)
ISBN: 979-8-7652-5001-3 (e)

Library of Congress Control Number: 2024903981

Balboa Press rev. date: 04/02/2024

DEDICATION

TO ERIC, LEO & NICOLE
Your existence gave me the gift of clarity.

TO SERGEI
Your love sent me into euphoric transcendence.

TO DR. SOHEILA NOORBAKHSH
Your wisdom led me to myself.

AUTHOR'S NOTE

Dear Reader,

This is the story about a heroine's journey. The road back to identity. Separation, initiation and return to self. The sinister price we pay for becoming estranged with our own inner world. It is a reflection on the urgency for reconciliation with self, for the entrapment does not have to be eternal.

In these pages, I hope you find the full spectrum of emotions that the human body and mind are capable of experiencing ... passion, rhapsody, euphoria, rage, courage, hope, fury and an awestruck revelation...THAT OUR VISIBILITY IS NOT NEGOTIABLE.

With infinite love,
Mary Terterov

CONTENTS

Part III Freedom

PART I

Hostage

What happens when people create a world we did not want … when they penetrate our minds & hearts?

ONCE UPON A GIRL

Once upon a time I was a little girl.
I believed everything
And everyone.

Then,
One day,
I found myself the toy of many sinister men.

Resourceful, fertile wife
Obedient, docile daughter
A demure woman with so much brain and so little awareness.

Suddenly,
I pranced off into the moonlight.
Blinded,
Lost,
Many wrong turns,
I ended up in the companionship of bottles and barricades

When the handsome masks came off,
I saw Monsters.
They were all the same.

Each salivating for a piece of my soul
That they would later maim...

BROKEN BOAT EMPIRE

He built an empire
While my soul starved at home

He pleased the whole world
While the casualties got stoned

Decades melted
Time never stopped
And he's still here
Angry with his manly broken heart

It's a dead end
Round and round we go.
When will he realize …
We're both rowing on a broken boat

CLOSED DOORS

His heart is always closed
just like his door.

There isn't even a doorknob.

HUMAN CARGO

Radio turned up
Silence invited
My presence uninvited

I was just a UPS box you had to drop off on a street corner.

SHEDDING

I shed the layers of my authentic self around you.

Is that your fault,
or mine?

INNOCENT BREASTS &
INSATIABLE BEASTS

My sensuality beaten out of me
To save my innocent, tender breasts
To protect my holy vagina

And all for what?
For that one lucky ravenous beast

To give him the opportunity to annihilate me
So he can enjoy the dominance of breaking my walls
And have the glory of watching my facial expression
as he pillages an unconquered village
Relishing the twists and turns
in all the dark corners inside of me

And all for what?
Even my virginity isn't enough.

LORD OF THE LIES

Sometimes we become so accustomed to the lies
that we start resenting the truth.

DINNER IS SERVED

His eyes looked like glazed donuts
Glossy
Removed
Possessed

Her eyes looked
Tired
Terrified
Intentionally clueless

Eating dinner together feels like chewing sharp glass
and having to smile after we swallow =)

VIRTUOUS VIRGINS & WHORES

They raised us as Virgin Daughters
Yet told our brothers to be Promiscuous Whores

Then society asked those promiscuous whores to marry those
virgin daughters …
And to be happy …
In holy matrimony…

And to love monogamy…
at least in theory ;)

THE STARVING RICH

All that fortune
And he's $till such an unfortunate man.

All that money
And he's $till starving.

UNDER SIEGE

"HANDS UP" –

"PUT YOUR WEAPONS DOWN"

They Said.

My body was under siege,
But even worse...
My brain was under social surrender

MARRIED YOUNG

They married a virgin
But the most virgin part of me was my
mind.

SAD MANSION

Big mansion
Rooms filled with hate

No love songs playing
Dead leaves by the gate

SHATTERED

Some days
I cannot offer you my most dignified or graceful self

All I can offer is pieces of broken glass
As I refuse to reunite with the rest of the shatter

HOSTAGE OF GREED

He put me on a barren canoe filled with cash
And pushed me into the middle of the sea
And walked away ...

F A R

F A R

A W A Y

Tornadoes of silence
Rivers of guilt

I got to shore penniless
And then he punished me
for being a victim of his own greed

His eyes are shut
His heart is closed

He weaponized his wrath
And seized me hostage to his own life

I was running towards and away from him all at the same time
Yet living under his leaking roof

MY SCHEMING SAVIOR

My Savior told me to get an education
But all he really wanted was an extravagant, wingless bird

My Savior told me I could walk on my own
But then he gently kicked a wheelchair to my knees

My Savior told me to open my big brown eyes
But then he delicately blindfolded me
With his soft, nimble fingers

He reached in and took my soul
Because clearly my soul was for the taking.

RUN

When you run
does your soul run with you ...

Or do you leave it behind?

PART II

Assault

What if we have achieved everything we set out to do but it has come at great sacrifice to our souls?

NOT YOURS

My body is not your ship
to anchor and sail at your leisure.

My mind is not your possession
to buy and sell.

My soul is not your toy
to fiddle with and break.

LOUD SILENCE

The louder the silence
the worthier I am to you.

MISMATCH

My body is tired
because it doesn't match my soul

THE DIFFERENCE

He has sex with my body
I have sex with his soul

PEACEFUL WAR

Negotiating a peace treaty with you
means waging war with myself

DECORATIVE DIPLOMA

Dime for dime
Penny for penny
You paid for my education
Yet refused to offer me a seat at your own table

Buttttttt…………..
The walls do look pretty damn nice
with all the diplomas on it, don't they?

They match the color of your ego

DIRTY SACRED SECRETS

Secrets Secrets
Dirty dirty secrets

They live inside my pores
And crawl inside my heart

Secrets Secrets
Dirty dirty secrets

Big or small
They're my precious darling secrets

So warm
So cozy
Come sit with me, you filthy little secrets

Join me here, join me there
Be my companion you flirty little secrets

Mama told me, no more secrets!
Too much blood
Too much shame
No more grimy slimy secrets

But ... who am I ...
Without these sacred secrets?

FOREIGN COUNTRY

Interacting with you
feels like being a foreigner in my own country.

DEVOURED

I had to run away to the mountains.
I had to run away from the life I built with my own two hands.

And when I returned,
I purged out all the humane pieces of me
so that I could continue to relentlessly devour the world.

But in the End,

The world devoured Me.

KEYLESS CAGE

I waged war
Against myself
On my own territory

I purchased the cage
Held myself prisoner
Set fire to my rage

Then one day
I started to look for the key
To let myself out

And then the epiphany came:

I was prisoner of a keyless cage.

3 QUESTIONS

New soul
Old soul
New soul
Old soul
New soul
Old soul
Which one am I?

Good girl
Bad girl
Good girl
Bad girl
Good girl
Bad girl
Which one am I?

Dead
Alive
Dead
Alive
Dead
Alive
Which one am I?

PART III

freedom

*What if we freed ourselves but didn't realize
how far we could truly take that freedom?*

CORONATION

I crowned myself
And hosted my own opulent coronation.

The most important people were invited...
Me,
Me, &
Me

UNFOLDING

Did someone fold me up
into a perfectly poised origami?
A swan, maybe?

My flaps,
O how they yearn to be unfolded...

The corners of my existence begging for thrilling wrinkles
The edges crying for the celebration of torn lines

Unfold,
my darling
Keep unfolding

RECKLESSLY ALIGNED

Sometimes being reckless
Aligns us with who we really are.

MY INTOXICATING MUSE

The first time I saw her
She was sitting at a café.

The contours of her face, simple yet complicated
The look in her eyes, friendly yet removed
The shape of her smile, inviting yet fleeting

But then,
I saw her soul.
J-a-g-g-e-d, beautiful edges
Dark, intoxicated madness,
the kind you don't want to escape

She dances through life even when the stage is burning
Sings as the ceilings collapse
Her world moves at the speed of lightening
Yet, she is profoundly ...
still.

I see her when I bleed
I see her when I soar
I see her when I cry
It's never enough, even when I get more

I'm in love with her dear soul
God help me, I couldn't love her more

FEARLESS DIMENSIONS

Her heart dances inside of mine
The truth slips off her tongue fearlessly
She lives deliberately in her own dimension
And if I'm lucky enough, she might look in my direction

NO ONE'S SACRIFICIAL LAMB

I won't sacrifice myself in the name of blood relationships.

STAY, COME, LEAVE

Your money made her Stay
Your money made the other one Come
But your money makes me want to LEAVE

SPECIAL

I know how to make other people feel special
But the real question is ...

Do I have the capacity to make myself feel special?

DON'T NEED EYES TO SEE

This girl I know
She can blindly see.

But me,
as for me?
Little old me ...
With perfect eyes I stood in front of a grandiose oasis
That I could hardly see.

So she just took the lead.

With no vision, she can blindly see.
She can see you
She can see me
And she can see everything in between

Her eyes SMELL the ravishing trees
Her eyes FEEL the stroke of the wind
Her eyes HEAR the nuzzling birds
Her eyes DISCERN more than your heart ever could

She leaned in and whispered to me:
You do not need those pretty eyes to see.

FANTASY

She was a fantasy that never was.

A story in my head.
Invading my mind.
Corrupting my soul.

A fantasy that could never be.
And now she stands in front me...
Ordering a cup of coffee.

Rejected. Like a sharp object shredding my skin.

She is a fantasy
Residing everywhere
but mostly nowhere.

TRUE LOVE

in my most basic form
he cherished me

SOUL PRESENCE

I'm physically here
I'm physically there
I'm physically everywhere

My feet touch the ground
But I can't find my soul
How did it leave me?
Where did it go?

I feel physically present,
But when will my soul arrive?

LET HIM SINK

I have to release you
And drop you to the depths of the deepest ocean
Because your weight is too burdensome

If I don't let you go
We'll both sink

INFINITE GROWTH

Are you in my way
or am I in yours?

Did I give you too much access to my life?
Too much access in between my legs?

Did you forget you were a beggar?
Begging to be saved
Begging for your next emotional high
Begging for someone to throw in a fishing pole
To bait in your own salvation

Was I the beggar's fool?
Or maybe you were part of my infinite growth?

So,
I think I want to say THANK YOU.

KEEP LICKING

I want to lick your magic
Like salt on a tequila rim

To savor it with each gulp
To let it burn the dead parts of me
And to set off rockets that were itching to be launched

To let it travel up and down my insides
Each naughty splash dancing in my heart

And to forget just enough
And to remember just enough
But not everything
Because the magic we chase is fleeting

Keep licking my friend.

ABOUT THE AUTHOR

MARY TERTEROV is a true Cali girl who loves to write poetry, novellas and short stories under the golden sun. With a Juris Doctorate degree and experience in criminal and civil litigation, this mama of three is an attorney gone rogue. Mary loves to compete in amateur Latin ballroom competitions, train for marathons and is the ultimate classical literature junkie. She also hosts an online blog featuring short articles focused on the human condition and the friction between our internal and external desires.

Find her at: www.YourGoToMama.com
IG Handle: mary_terterov

ACKNOWLEDGMENTS

It is rare to find a friend who sees you even when you don't see yourself. That friend who asks courageous questions that shift the course of your life. To **Tina Esrailian**, you are an extra-terrestrial creature. A sister. A confidant. With your delicate essence, you picked me up by my collar and placed me exactly where I needed to be … at a writer's retreat amongst kindred spirit. You made space for me and helped me carve out the most honest moments of my life. Thank you for reminding me that everything is at stake.

There are few people in life who willingly grant you permission to fail. To **Mick Thyer**, my Editor, who not only granted that permission but invited me to take the big leap into the abyss of my subconscious. Thank you for reminding me to be provocative in my writing and to expose the human condition without attachments to external outcomes.

A CONVERSATION WITH MARY TERTEROV

Reader's Circle: What is representative of the heroine's journey?

Mary Terterov: This journey is about the road back to identity, to ourselves, and to that child that was taken away. This process involves separation, initiation and a return to self.

RC: What is our own personal participation in this struggle?

MT: Often, we are fighting a battle we are not even conscious of. We become prisoners in our own world and find ourselves asking for permission to live. However, the cage was always open. The door never even had a lock and key.

RC: What is society's role in the protagonist's invisibility?

MT: There is a struggle for identity and visibility, especially in a male dominated society. The heroine is born invisible, and later becomes visible as an object of desire. However, her visibility belongs to 'them.' And so she begins to fight to earn agency over her own life. But often, that agency is earned by the heroine rejecting the feminine in favor of the masculine. She may still be tied to the feminine, but she increasingly resents that attachment.

RC: How does the heroine become a spiritual warrior?

MT: By reconciling with her feminine side and becoming visible on her own terms. She does this by learning the delicate art of balance and how to have the patience for the slow, subtle integration of the feminine and masculine aspects of her nature.

RC: Why does the protagonist's desire exist in secrecy?

MT: Whenever the heroine owns herself, it feels secretive because desire tarnishes her innocence. When innocence is remembered, any desire is risky. Unspoiled purity, by definition, will always be at odds with humanity's innate desires and fantasies. And the true irony is, even the virgin is eventually taken and touched.

RC: What are emotions women are often disallowed from feeling?

MT: Desire, wants, needs, curiosity, truth, power and a longing to change.

RC: What is the role of innocence?

MT: Innocence has been heavily commodified by society and weaponized as a vehicle for blackmail and control. It's also a tool for families to fulfill a social prophecy. It becomes the currency for a guaranteed "good girl" narrative. It's paradoxical that the preservation of innocence is achieved through the cruelty of adulthood.

RC: What are the landscapes at the heart of this book?

MT: Oceans, mountains, deserts, the female body, the female mind.

RC: What thematic settings parallel the heroine's entrapment of the female body and mind?

MT: The bedroom, the kitchen table, beneath the sheets, the metaphorical prison, mansions, and classrooms.

RC: What is at the core of this poetry collection?

MT: The power of the human spirit.

QUESTIONS FOR DISCUSSION

1. How do I recognize myself in this world?
2. How do I know who I am?
3. What theme do I value in life?
4. No choice is a choice. Agree or disagree?
5. What happens when 'choice' is taken away? When do I take it back?
6. Is it a sin to willfully destroy innocence?
7. How do I go about seeking validation?
8. What am I willing to sacrifice to earn back my visibility?
9. What do I want to shout out to the world?
10. What is the cost of my silence?